Reading/Writing Companion

Mc
Graw
Hill

Welcome to
WONDERS!

We are so excited about how much you will learn and grow this year! We're here to help you set goals for your learning.

You will build on what you already know and learn new things every day.

You will read a lot of fun stories and interesting texts on different topics.

You will write about the texts you read. You will also write texts of your own. You will do research as well.

You will explore new ideas by reading different texts.

Each week, we will set goals on the My Goals page. Here is an example:

I can read and understand texts.

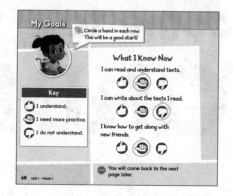

As you read and write, you will learn skills and strategies to help you reach your goals.

You will think about your learning and sometimes circle a hand to show your progress.

Check In

Here are some questions you can ask yourself.

- Did I understand the task?
- Was it easy?
- Was it hard?
- What made it hard?

It is okay if I need more practice. The most important thing is to do my best and keep learning!

If you need more help, you can choose what to do.

- Talk to a friend or teacher.

- Use an Anchor Chart.

- Choose a center activity.

At the end of each week, you will complete a fun task to show what you have learned.

Then you will return to your My Goals page and think about your learning.

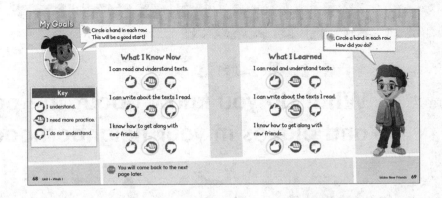

Unit 4 Around the Neighborhood

The Big Idea

Week 1 • Time for Work

Digital Tools Find this eBook and other resources at: my.mheducation.com

Week 2 • Meet Your Neighbors

Week 3 • Pitch In

Extended Writing

Personal Narrative

Connect and Reflect

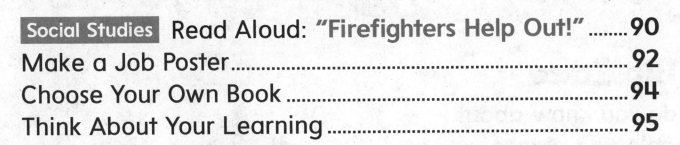

Purestock/SuperStock

Unit 4

Around the Neighborhood

The Big Idea

What do you know about the people and places in your neighborhood?

 Talk about what the neighbors in the picture are doing.

 Circle the neighbors who are playing together.

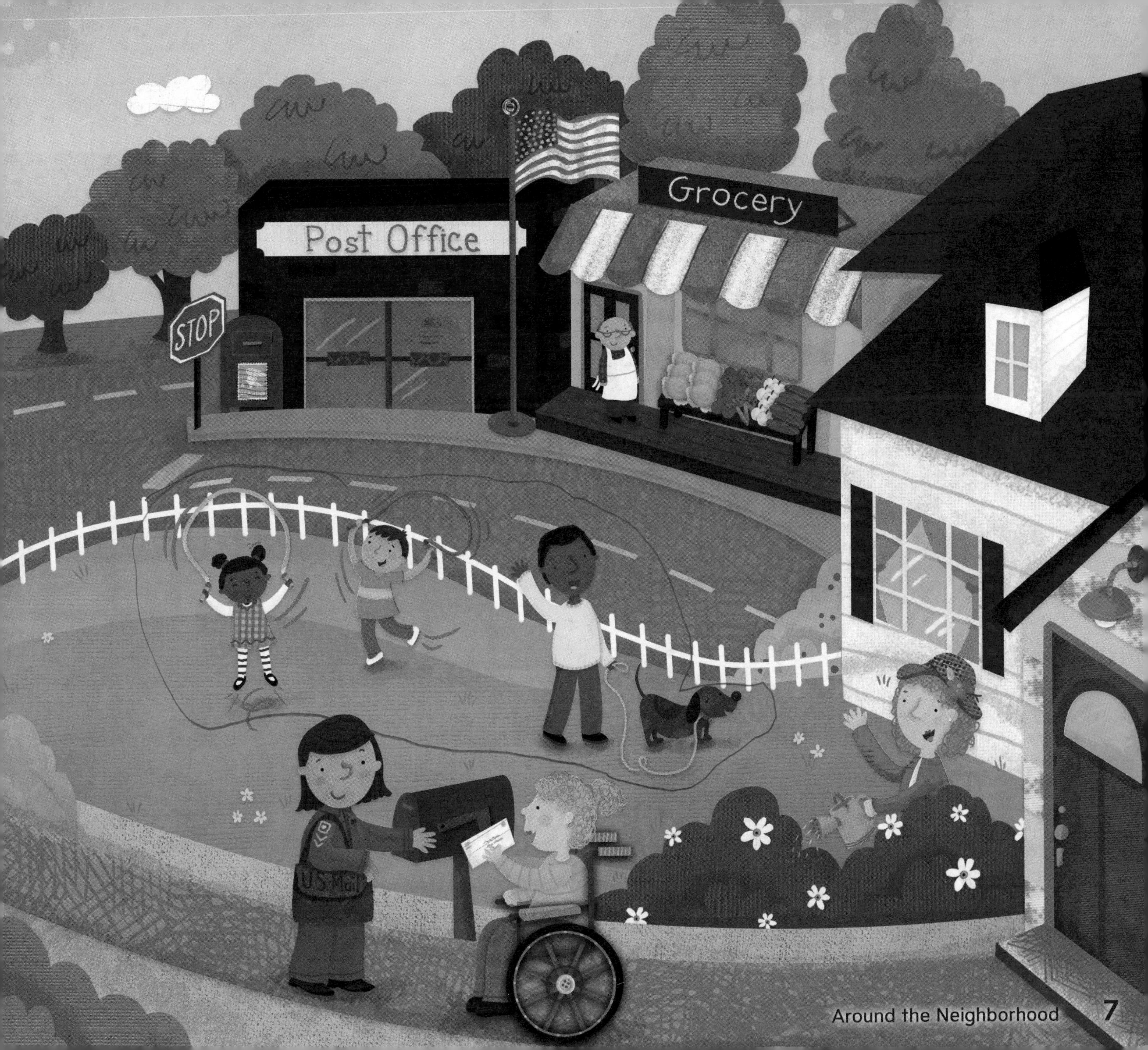
Post Office
Grocery
STOP
U.S. Mail

Build Vocabulary

 Talk about things people use to do their jobs. What are some words that name these things?

 Draw a picture of one of these things.

Write the word.

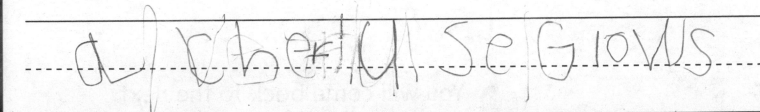

Tanya Constantine/Blend Images/Getty Images

My Goals

 Circle a hand in each row. It will be fun to learn more.

What I Know Now

I can read and understand texts.

I can write about the texts I read.

I know what people use to do their jobs.

Key

 I understand.

 I need more practice.

 I do not understand.

 You will come back to the next page later.

Circle a hand in each row.
What are you getting better at?

What I Learned

I can read and understand texts.

I can write about the texts I read.

I know what people use to do their jobs.

Retell the nonfiction text.

 Write about the text.

Whose Shoes?
Stephen R. Swinburne

An important fact I learned is

 Text Evidence

Page

An interesting part of the text is

 Text Evidence

Page

Talk about special clothing that workers wear.

 Draw and **write** about a worker who wears special clothes.

This worker wears
_____

- -

_____

Details in the words and photos in a nonfiction text give information about the **topic.**

 Listen to and **look** at part of the text.

 Talk about the topic and details.

 Write two details.

Two details are

1. _____

_____

2. _____

Draw one detail you wrote about.

 Talk about how the words and photos help you learn information.

Check In

Listen to and **look** at pages 13–18.

 Talk about how each question has an answer.

 Draw the answer to the question on page 13.

Look at pages 25–30.

 Talk about how the author shows that each shoe goes with a worker.

 Draw and **write** about a shoe from the text.

This shoe is good because

_____

- - - - - - - - - - - - - - - - - -

_____

🔍 **Find Text Evidence**

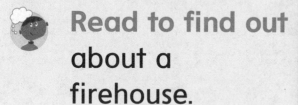

Read to find out about a firehouse.

Circle and read the word **you.**

Tom On Top!

Can you see a ?
firehouse

Find Text Evidence

 Ask questions you may have about the text as you read. This can help you learn information.

 Read each sentence. Point to and name the first letter and end mark in each sentence.

I can see a 🚒 .
fire truck

I can see a  firefighter .

Shared Read

🔍 **Find Text Evidence**

✏️ **Circle** what is red on page 22.

✏️ **Underline** the lowercase letters on page 23.

I can see a 🧯. hose

I can see a hat .

Shared Read

🔍 **Find Text Evidence**

✏️ **Circle** words that have the same middle sound as **mop**.

👥 **Retell** the text. Use the words and photos to help you.

I can see a pot.

I can see Tom on top!

Paired Selection

 Look at the photos. What tools do firefighters use?

 Talk about the tools you see in the big and little photos.

 Draw a line from the tool in the little photo to the same tool in the big photo.

Quick Tip

You can use these sentence starters:

Firefighters ____.

They use ____.

hose   boots

helmet

Talk about the tools in the little photos. Choose one to write about.

Write how this tool helps firefighters.

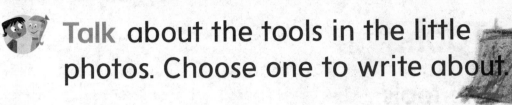

This tool is

Firetuuk

This tool helps firefighters

save peple

down the ladder.

Baea them Back

Talk About It

Why does the author include photos and lab

28 Unit 4

Workers and Their Tools

Step 1 Talk about jobs and the tools workers use. Choose a job.

Step 2 Write a question about the tools a worker needs to do that job.

_____

- -

_____

- -

_____

Step 3 Look at books or use the Internet. You can also talk with a worker who does that job.

Step 4 Draw and write about what you learned.

_____

- -

_____

Step 5 Choose a good way to present your work.

 Talk about what this worker is doing. What tools is he using?

 Compare these tools to the tools you read about in other texts this week.

syolacan/E+/Getty Images

Quick Tip

You can use these sentence starters:

The worker is ____.

Tools from other texts are ____.

Write About a Job

1 Think about the texts you read. What did you learn about things people use to do their jobs?

2 Choose two jobs that you read about. **Draw** the workers and the things they need to do their jobs.

3 Write about what would happen if the workers traded their tools. Use words that you learned this week.

Think about what you learned this week. Turn to page 11.

Build Knowledge

Essential Question Who are your neighbors?

Build Vocabulary

 Talk about who your neighbors are. What are some words that name different neighbors?

 Draw a picture of a neighbor.

 Write the word.

_____

- -

_____

My Goals

Circle a hand in each row. Whatever you know is okay!

What I Know Now

I can read and understand texts.

I can write about the texts I read.

I know who my neighbors are.

Key

 I understand.

 I need more practice.

 I do not understand.

 You will come back to the next page later.

Circle a hand in each row.
It is okay if you need more practice.

What I Learned

I can read and understand texts.

I can write about the texts I read.

I know who my neighbors are.

Retell the realistic fiction story.

 Write about the story.

A paleta is good because

‑‑

Text Evidence

Page

This is realistic fiction because

‑‑

Text Evidence

Page

Talk about what the girl, her family, and her neighbors do with a paleta.

 Draw and **write** about what you would do with a paleta.

I would

_____

- -

_____

The **main character** is who a fiction story is mostly about. The **setting** is where the story takes place.

 Listen to and **look** at the story.

 Talk about the main character and the setting.

 Write about the main character.

The main character is

_____

- - - - - - - - - - - - - - - - - - -

_____

_____

- - - - - - - - - - - - - - - - - - -

_____

Draw and **write** about the setting.

The neighborhood is

_____

- -

_____

Check In

Listen to and **look** at page 27.

 Talk about how the girl's words help you see, feel, and smell the roses.

 Draw and **write** about the roses. Use words from the story to help you.

The roses are

Listen to and **look** at pages 27–31.

 Draw and **write** about the character who is telling the story. What might she say about where she lives?

I like where I live because

_____

- -

_____

Find Text Evidence

 Ask questions you may have before reading the story. Then read to find the answers.

 Circle and read the word **Do**.

Sid

Do Sid and Mom like it?

Find Text Evidence

Circle an object on this page whose name begins with the same sound as **dip**.

Underline words that tell what Dan can do.

Sid and Mom do like it!

Dan can tap, tap on a .
door

🔍 **Find Text Evidence**

✏️ ○ **Circle** the picture of Dot on page 46.

✏️ ┈ **Underline** words on page 47 that begin with the same sound as **did**.

Dot can tap, tap on a .
door

Dot and Dan can sip.

Find Text Evidence

Circle words that end with the same sound as **sad**.

Retell the story. Use the words and pictures to help you.

Tod can tap, tap on a .
door

Sid and Tod pat a .
ball

Paired Selection

 Listen to pages 33–35.

Quick Tip

You can use these sentence starters:

The name of the character is ____.

One of the places he goes is ____.

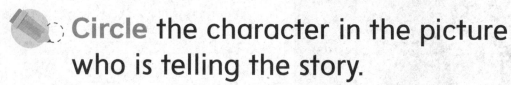 **Circle** the character in the picture who is telling the story.

 Write his name. Tell what he likes to do.

_____

- -

_____

Talk about the places where Caleb goes in his neighborhood.

 Draw a place where Caleb goes. Show what he does there.

 Write About It

Caleb wrote a personal narrative about himself and what he likes to do. Now write about yourself and what you like to do.

Neighbors Interview

Step 1 **Talk** about different things neighbors do together.

Step 2 **Write** a question about things neighbors do together.

_____

- -

_____

_____

- -

_____

Step 3 **Ask** classmates and neighbors your question.

Step 4 Draw what you learned.

Step 5 Choose a good way to present your work.

 Talk about what these neighbors are doing together. How are they having fun?

 Compare these neighbors to the neighbors in *What Can You Do with a Paleta?*

Quick Tip

You can use these sentence starters:

These neighbors are ____.

The neighbors in the story are ____.

kali9/E+/Getty Images

LAFS K.RL.3.9, K.RI.3.9, K.SL.I.I.b

Make a Neighbor Book

1 **Think** about the texts you read. What did you learn about neighbors?

2 **Talk** to a neighbor. **Draw** two things you learned about your neighbor.

3 **Write** words that tell about your pictures. Use words that you learned this week.

Think about what you learned this week. Turn to page 35.

Build Knowledge

? Essential Question How can people help to make their community better?

Build Vocabulary

 Talk about how people can help make their community better. What words tell about how people can help?

 Draw a picture of one of the words.

 Write the word.

My Goals

Circle a hand in each row.
It is important to do your best.

What I Know Now

I can read and understand texts.

I can write about the texts I read.

I know how people can help make my community better.

STOP You will come back to the next page later.

Key

 I understand.

 I need more practice.

 I do not understand.

Circle a hand in each row. Keep up the good work!

What I Learned

I can read and understand texts.

I can write about the texts I read.

I know how people can help make my community better.

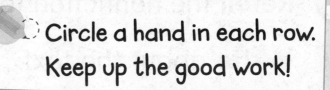

Retell the nonfiction text.

 Write about the text.

An interesting fact I learned is

_____

- - - - - - - - - - - - - - - - - - -

_____

_____ **Text Evidence**

- - - - - - - - - - - - - - - - - - - Page

_____

I know this text is nonfiction because **Text Evidence**

_____ Page

- - - - - - - - - - - - - - - - - - -

_____

Talk about workers who help your community.

 Draw a worker who helps.

 Share how the worker you drew helps your community.

Details give us information about the order of events, or time order, in a text. The words *first, next,* **and** *last* **tell the order.**

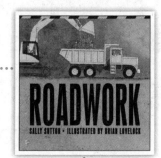

 Listen to and **look** at part of the text.

 Talk about what happens *first, next,* and *last.*

 Draw what happens.

First

Next

Last

Listen to and **look** at pages 14–15.

 Talk about the sound words the author uses. How do these words help you know what the workers are doing?

 Write your ideas.

The words help me know

_____

- -

_____

- -

_____

Listen to and **look** at page 32.
Why do you think the author added
this page?

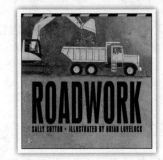

 Talk about the different machines
and facts about them.

 Draw one of the machines.
Show a fact about it.

 **Find Text Evidence**

Ask questions about the story before you read. Then read to find out what the mom and girl can do.

Circle and read the words **and, go,** and **to**.

I Can, You Can!

Mom and I go to a .
beach

Shared Read

🔍 **Find Text Evidence**

⬡ **Circle** what the girl can pat, pat, pat.

⬡ **Underline** and read the word **you**.

I can pat, pat, pat on top.

Can you pat it?

Find Text Evidence

Circle the picture of Stan.

Underline the word that begins with the same sounds as **spin**.

I can tip, tip it on top.

Stan can spot it.

 **Find Text Evidence**

Circle the word that begins with the same sounds as **snip**.

Retell the story. Use the words and pictures to help you.

I can pat, pat, pat on top.

We can do it in a snap!

Look at the photos. How can people work together to plant a garden?

First they dig. Next they plant seeds. Then they water.

 Talk about the words that help you know the order of each step.

 Circle the words that tell the order.

Listen to page 36.

 Talk about what happens when the vegetables are ready to pick.

 Write what happens last.

Last

_____

- - - - - - - - - - - - - - - - - - -

_____

- - - - - - - - - - - - - - - - - - -

_____

Talk About It

Talk about ways people can help make a garden. How can a garden help a community?

Neil Guegan/Image Source

Interview About School

Step 1 **Talk** about ways you can make your school community better.

Step 2 **Write** a question about things you can do to help your school.

_____

- -

_____

_____

- -

_____

Step 3 **Ask** classmates and school workers your question.

Step 4 **Draw** and **write** about what you learned.

We can make our school better by

_____

- -

_____

Step 5 **Choose** a good way to present your work.

Talk about how these people pitch in to help their community.

 Compare how these people help their community to how the workers in *Roadwork* help their community.

Quick Tip

You can use these sentence starters:

These people help by ___.

The people in the text help by ___.

These people donate clothing and other items to people who need them.

JUPITERIMAGES/Brand X/Alamy

Make a Community Quilt

1 **Think** about the texts you read. What did you learn about how you can help make your community better?

2 **Make** a quilt square. **Draw** one way you can make your community better.

3 **Write** about the way you can make it better. Use words that you learned this week.

Think about what you learned this week. Turn to page 59.

Writing and Grammar

Yoshi

I wrote a personal narrative. It is a story that tells about something that happened to me.

Personal Narrative

My personal narrative tells about an event that was special to me.

Student Model

My Mystery Trip

My Uncle Shiro took me to the airport.

But we did not get on a plane.

We watched gigantic jets land and take off.

It was loud.

I had so much fun!

Genre Study

 Talk about what makes Yoshi's writing a personal narrative.

 Ask any questions you have about personal narratives.

 Circle how Yoshi feels about the trip.

Plan

 Talk about something that happened to you.

 Draw what happened.

Write what your personal narrative is about.

My personal narrative is about

_____

- -

_____

 Draw a detail that happened.

Draft

Read Yoshi's draft of his personal narrative.

Student Model

A Trip to the Airport

My Uncle Shiro took me to the airport.

But we did not get on a plane.

We watched jets.

I had so much fun!

Time Order
I put the events in order.

I included a detail that tells more about what happened.

Writing Skill
I used my Word Bank to help me spell this word.

Ken Cavanagh/McGraw-Hill Education

Your Turn

Begin to write your personal narrative in your writer's notebook. Use your ideas from pages 82-83.

Revise and Edit

Think about how Yoshi revised
and edited his personal narrative.

I made sure
to spell the word
the correctly.

Student Model

I wrote a
better title.

My Mystery Trip

My Uncle Shiro took me to the airport.

But we did not get on a plane.

We watched gigantic jets land and take off.

It was loud.

I had so much fun!

I added a **sentence**.
It tells a complete idea.

I added an **adjective**.

I added details to
make my writing
more interesting.

Ken Cavanagh/McGraw-Hill Education

Grammar

- A **sentence** is a group of words that tells a complete idea.

- An **adjective,** or describing word, tells more about a noun.

I added more details to my picture.

Your Turn

Revise and edit your personal narrative. Be sure to use complete sentences and adjectives. Use your checklist.

Share and Evaluate

 Practice presenting your work with a partner. Take turns.

 Present your work. Then use this checklist.

Review Your Work	Yes	No
Writing		
I wrote a personal narrative.	☐	☐
I added details.	☐	☐
I used my Word Bank to help spell words.	☐	☐
Speaking and Listening		
I spoke in a loud, clear voice.	☐	☐
I asked questions.	☐	☐

Talk with a partner about your writing.

Write about your work.

What did you do well in your writing?

_____

- -

_____

_____

- -

_____

What do you need to work on?

_____

- -

_____

Find Out About Firefighters

 Listen to "Firefighters Help Out!"

 Talk about different jobs firefighters do.

 Draw one job that a firefighter does.

Compare the ways firefighters help in a community.

Write about one way they help.

Quick Tip

You can use these sentence starters:

One way firefighters help is ____.

Another way they help is ____.

Firefighters help by

_____

- -

_____

_____

- -

_____

Connect to Social Studies

Make a Job Poster

 Talk about different jobs people do and the tools they use.

What to Do

1. **Draw** a job that people do.

   Show the tools the worker uses.

2. **Add** details to your poster.

3. **Write** a caption for your poster.

4. **Share** and compare your poster.

You Need

pencil

crayons

(bkg)arigato/Shutterstock, (stethoscope)Matin/Shutterstock.com, (pencil)Africa Studio/Shutterstock.com, (crayons)bogdan ionescu/Shutterstock.com, (tools)Mark Steinmetz/McGraw-Hill Education

Choose Your Own Book

Minutes I Read

 Write the title of the book.

 Tell a partner why you want to read it.
Then read the book.

 Write your opinion of the book.

Think About Your Learning

Think about what you learned in this unit.

 **Share** one thing you did well.

 Write one thing you want to get better at.

_____

- -

_____

- -

_____

Share a goal you have with your partner.

My Sound-Spellings

Aa a apple	**Bb** b bat	**Cc** c ck k camel	**Dd** d dolphin	**Ee** e egg	**Ff** f fire	**Gg** g guitar
Hh h_ hippo	**Ii** i insect	**Jj** j jump	**Kk** c k ck koala	**Ll** l lemon	**Mm** m map	**Nn** n nest
Oo o octopus	**Pp** p piano	**Qq** qu_ queen	**Rr** r rose	**Ss** s sun	**Tt** t turtle	**Uu** u umbrella
Vv v volcano	**Ww** w_ window	**Xx** x box	**Yy** y_ yo-yo	**Zz** z _s zipper		

Aa Bb Cc Dd Ee

Ff Gg Hh Ii Jj

Kk Ll Mm Nn

Oo Pp Qq Rr

Ss Tt Uu Vv

Ww Xx Yy Zz